The Earth is our spaceship, sailing through space.
It is just right for us to live on.
We can live nearly everywhere on the Earth.

The north and south poles of the
Earth are covered with thick ice.
Nobody wants to live there.
If all the ice melted, the Earth
would be covered with water.

The Bible tells the story of Noah.
When the Earth was covered with water,
Noah built a boat and rescued all the
animals from the floods.

The Earth would not be a good
place to live on if we were closer
to the sun.
The seas would dry up.

If the Earth was too far from
the sun, everywhere would be
gloomy and cold.
The seas would freeze.

If the moon was too close to
the Earth, giant waves would sweep
the land.

Cracks would appear in the Earth, and volcanoes would explode.

The moon might explode and rain
pieces down on the Earth.

One way the Earth might die would be if a new Ice Age came. Everywhere would be covered in thick ice.

If the Earth stopped turning round,
one side would always face the sun.
It would always be daytime and
too hot to live.

The other side of the Earth would
always face the dark of space.
It would always be night-time and
too cold to live.

In a famous story by H. G. Wells, the Earth is attacked by invaders from Mars.

The invasion is stopped when the
invaders die from Earth diseases
like mumps and measles.

Life on Earth would die if we did
not take care of the Earth and keep it clean.

Do not worry, life on Earth will not die.
The Earth will last for millions of years
if we take care of it.

The Earth is our spaceship.
It is the only one we have.
Take care of it.